AF394424

AURORA

ALL MY DEMONS GREETING ME AS A FRIEND

mf
Moderato
f risoluto.

In case of loss, please return to:

____

____

____

____

As a reward: $ _______________________________

Being human and coming to peace with all the demons
we surround ourselves with, sometimes unwillingly.

Eat breakfast with them.
Dance with them.
Quarrel with them.
Talk to them.
And make sure they know their visit is only temporary.
And when the time is due, let them go.
And now at least, you can part as friends.
They used to be a part of you, after all.

ALL MY DEMONS GREETING ME AS A FRIEND

The firstborn.

If I were a king, this album would be the heir to the throne.
If I were a teacher this album would be my first apprentice.
If I were a God this album would be the first of words, and eventually they
would become all too powerful and most likely interpreted wrongly.

But I'm none of those things.
So this album is simply what it is.

An album written long before I knew it was going to be one.
Which I find rather lovely.

I began writing around the age of six. I had no intentions with my writing besides
the fact that it made me feel heavenly. I wrote purely because it made life
seem meaningful. And I needed life to be meaningful.

Because then meaning would live beyond love, and hope, birth and growth,
and shed its light on things like sadness, and envy, grief and death.
Sometimes writing music would make my sadness grow wings,
and suddenly all the emotions my body harboured would leave me
for a moment, whilst I stood on the ground and observed it.
It made me feel like I could be larger than my sadness.
And bigger than my anxiousness.

And if these heavy emotions could inspire and become something as beautiful as music,
I felt like I could learn to appreciate them as much as I appreciated joy.

And calm.

When it comes to emotions, I believe the distance
from them is as equally important as the closeness.
I believe it's important to both allow them in, and face them –
but also to remind ourselves that this might only be a temporary thing.

I always hoped that sadness would never have too much of an identity,
but rather something that sat within you as long as you allow it.

And of course, some types of sadness never disappear.
They remain in the back of our minds as long as we live.

Therefore, we need to learn how to live with them, and trust
that if the mark made on our souls will not change, we might.
If the sadness will not get smaller, then we will be larger.
Then suddenly the sadness isn't that big part of us anymore. Even if it's still there.

This is what *All My Demons Greeting Me as a Friend* was all about, to me.
If people befriend their own demons, face their fear, and cradle
their sorrow, we would learn to become more curious about all the
things that make us human, rather than staying fearful of them.

We learn to open up about it too, and together we may help each
other understand that we are much less alone than we thought.

I still believe the saddest lie we've ever been told is that we must go through
the darkness of life on our own. We keep it hidden, because we think the
world won't understand our shadow. But in reality, we all have shadows.
Everything we feel on this earth are universal feelings.

These feelings are meant to be shared. And heard. Seen.
These feelings are meant to be honoured.
A way to honour emotions.
Like laughter honours happiness.
And crying honours sadness.

Best of all, to both cry and laugh at the same time.
And you get to feel a bit mad. Which is also entirely human.

I knew when I started piecing this album together, I wanted it to feel entirely human.
Because for all the lovely people out there, including myself,
music can be such a wonderful friend in times of need.

I named my first album *All My Demons Greeting Me as a Friend* to help welcome the
sadness into our lives more as a friend than a part of you. Because I think we're
better at being good to our friends than we are at being good to ourselves.

Especially when we feel that we are made of things we dislike.
Like sadness.
Or fear.
Or cowardice.
Or insecurities.
Or the worst one of all, jealousy.

These were a lot of the thoughts swirling in my mind as I put this album together.
And because I knew that I would make many albums in my life,
I spent a lot of time wondering how to begin my path correctly.

How to introduce my music to whoever out there
might need it before they even knew I existed.
And it simply made sense.
Since I am not a king.
Or a teacher.
Or a God.

To introduce my songs as a friend to whoever out there might need it.
Once we learn to make friends with all the things we are made of,
the good and the bad, I think life becomes truly beautiful.
We become truly beautiful.
And not just briefly.

Thank you for lending me your ears, all these years.
It truly is the greatest gift I have ever received in my life.

it is strange
how we choose our
memories
I cant remember
how we met
but I remember
how you died
I can remember how you
fell and how

YOU HAVE CHANGED ME
YOU TOOK MY VOICE

PLEASE PLEASE DON'T MAKE ME INTO SOMETHING

BRYR DERE EGENTLIG DERE OM MEG?

Just let me die

CONFUSED

NOW I have lost myself

NOOOOOOOOOOOOOOO

I HATE EVERYONE

I AM I NOT IN MY MIND

LUCKY is DYING DYING.

HEY HIM

I hate my life

its Making me sick

COLD

JUST KILL ME NOW

TEARS they took my children sick

WHY

I. am. unhappy.

de sa de ville passe på at artister var lykkelig

this jeg føler meg is brukt. jeg er ikke not stolt about det music gjør

I am miserable

HOLD KJEFT DA

NE-I

jeg hater alle sammen

BUT i hate it i JUST DON'T LIKE IT

I DON'T WANT TO LIE

DIE av jeg DIE lengre

NOOO på at jeg glemte min egen stemme.

I'M TELLING 16

DIE lengre anymore Jes DIE lengre

jeg blot folk ta makt over hva som var mitt.

PEOPLE ARE

THIS IS TERRIBLE

GIE
ORCR
ATAN
ATAN

LOOKING FOR THE LOST BOOK

I have during the recent months been looking for
'the lost book.'

The one book that contains the part of my brain
that you might not hear in the music.

In my defence, the concept that came to life around
my first album was written over 12 years ago.
And I am not a stranger to losing things. Sadly.

But what I did find were all kinds of different,
less perfect books that contain many of the ideas
and thoughts I had during the process of writing
'All My Demons Greeting Me as a Friend'.

And that is precisely what you will find in this book.
A less aesthetic scramble of it all.
But equally as important.
Looking through my words, I was surprised by the emotions
they awakened.

I sat in my childhood room crying with the pages on my lap.
I was truly so sad back then, in my earlier years,
and I had almost completely forgotten.
Not only sad.
Happy too.
Bewildered and enchanted by the world.
But also terrified of the new world that had opened up for me
after I became an artist.

I remember trying to feel happiness from the things
I had been told were supposed to make you happy.
But I never did.
And I thought I was depressed.
Because so much of the success I was having
didn't make me feel anything.

Of course, now I know, it's the making of the music that
makes my heart tingle, not the reaction that it provokes.
Some things may excite me less than they excite other people.
And that is ok. Writing makes me excited.
Collecting moths and teeth makes me excited.
And this is something other people might not understand.
And that is ok too.

Luckily, people are built differently.
It makes the world so enticing.

I think it often is the case, that the people
who build their art need a lot of peace.
And a lot of shelter.
But you figure it out as you adapt
to the new world around you.
The silence isn't lost, simply because it is loud.
You just step into another room,
and it's like the noise never existed.

Now I know how to do that.
And doing what I do has become a thing I enjoy.
I enjoy people now.
And even the noise (sometimes).
But I also enjoy my solitude
and the silence that comes with it.

Ever since I released my first album,
life has been such a wonderful adventure.
And it's been so terrible too.

It's been both.
Which I think is good.

This might be the whole point of living. One cannot be happy
at all times, but one can be content. And hope the things we
mourn were worth the gift of loving them. Whilst learning to
let go, we then dare to make room for something new.

Yes, it is easier said than done.
I sometimes remember to do the things I tell my friends
to do, when life hurts. But not always.

It is hard work.
But it's very rewarding.

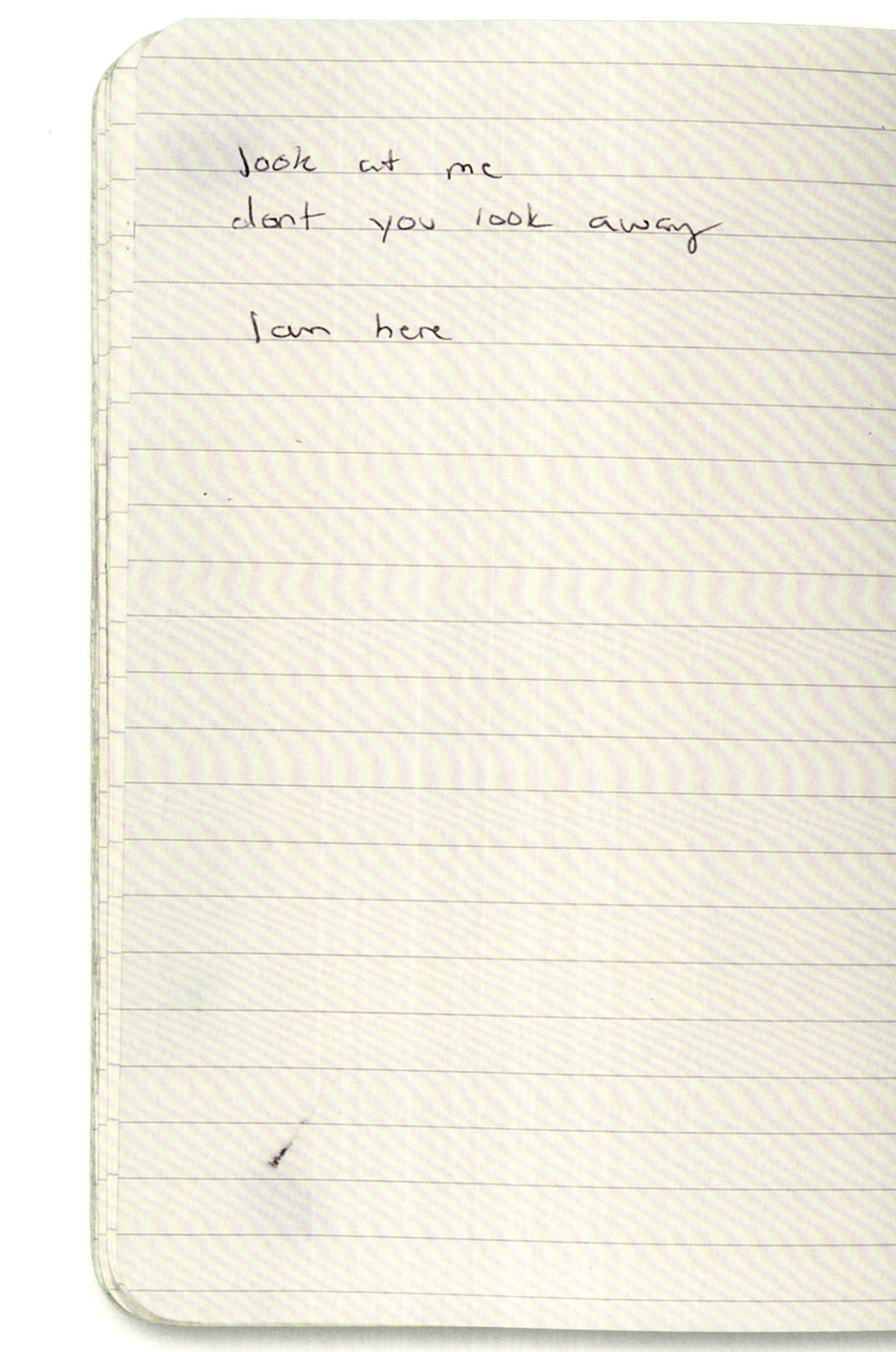
look at me
dont you look away

I am here

people around me
make so much
noise. I cant
hear my thoughts

I dont know if
I like it or
not.

I prefer
to be quiet.

prefer te
tint.

daydream.

I have never held much anger within me, but one thing that
always angered me was when people mistook my love of the
moth for love of the butterfly.
I always loved moths, from when I was a young child to now.
And I never cared much for the butterfly.

I felt like the butterfly always got the attention.
Butterflies are known for their colours, and the
transformation they symbolise holds great importance for people.
And I understand this. Transformation. Growth. Change.
It's a beautiful thing. The butterfly is good for the one
who needs a new beginning.
Or an escape from a former self.

But this is not what I needed.

Butterflies are associated with sunlight — they often come
around when the sun is there to warm your skin. And the
transformation they symbolise is out in the open for the
world to see, which makes it easy to notice and celebrate.

The moth on the other hand, is often overlooked and
forgotten. Moths often come around during the night, and
this nocturnal nature is associated with dark and the moon.
With the unknown.
I know in many cultures the moth is also associated with
death, or the dead.
Small messengers from the spirit world.

The moth is more mysterious. And whatever process it
symbolises seems to me to be more internal and hidden.
Like many important things of this world.
But even though the regular brown-winged moth might seem
dull to most, I can't help but admire their persistence.
They roam the night, and they always seem to hunt the light.
Even if it becomes the very trap that kills them.

I always found this so beautiful.
Sad.
And beautiful.

How something so ordinary and small
could be something so poetic.

That is why I always knew I wanted to be a moth on the cover
of 'All My Demons Greeting Me as a Friend'. To symbolise
the process of feeling small and invisible. A little lost
in the dark. But relentless. And poetic. And lovable.
It just takes the right eye to notice.

An ordinary brown-winged moth might not be grand,
but they know exactly who they are.
They are beautiful, not because the eye that observes them
deems them as beautiful, but simply because
they are a perfect little creation.
If I can see beauty in them,
I think I could find it in myself.

This would make it so much easier to live my life as myself.
On my own terms.
As then you cannot be bullied.
And you cannot be harmed.
Because you know who you are, and that is something
humans spend a whole lifetime trying to figure out.
During my search for
'the missing book' I found
these pictures in an old phone
I had left behind in a box that
hasn't been opened
in nearly a decade.

In the photograph you see a poem
written to the first moth
I ever collected.
I found it lying ever so
peacefully and dead,
in a window.
I named it Night Crawler.

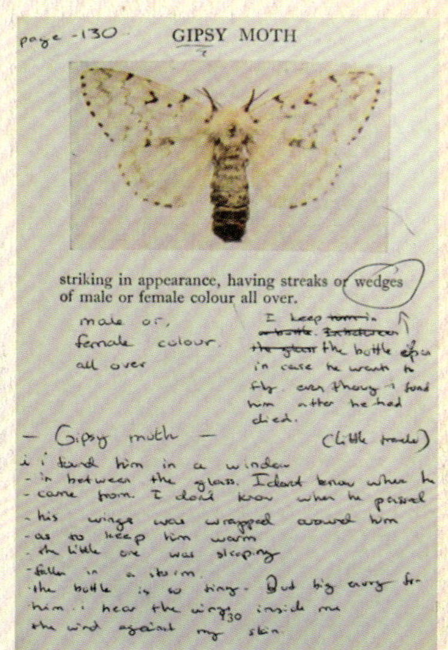

I keep the bottle open
in case he wants to fly
Even though I found him
after he had died

the bottle is so tiny
but big enoug for him
I hear the wings beside me
the wind against my skin

in every dream

NIGHT CRAWLER

I found him in a window
in between the glass
I don't know where he came from
don't know when he passed

The wings was wrapped around him
to keep his body warm
the little one is sleeping
fallen in a storm

i took him in my hands
I brought him home
i see him fly inside my head
i keep him in a bottle-glass
so I can see him from my bed
i'm not alone
is not alone

fig. 1.
fig. 2.
fig. 3.
fig. 4.
fig. 5.
fig. 6.

Bring me some hope.
If only a feather.
a feather who once belonged
to a bird.
I've never seen hope and
reality together
but its a botiful thing
as far as I haver heard

I was only elleven when I fell
and since that day I've
known that dark so well
and now I can't see
anything clear
there is no happy songs
for me to hear

an isolated soul
with no one else in sight to hear
the crying and the tears
the constant looming fear

His fam'ly and friends.
he knows he'll never see
again...
afraid to understand
that he loves another man

they say it is a sin.
they try to pull their hands apart
now nothing can repair
the war within his heart

-"the war of Love"
by AURORA c201

Once upon a time there was a man called "King Solomon"
He posessed a ring which could make the happiest man In the world sad, and the saddest man happy. on the ring these words were written.

"This too shall pass."

That is the way of life. In times of sadness, remember this. — but also in good times. Value life to the full.

Sometimes you find a piece of furniture that reminds you
of something magical. I found this old closet in a place
I cannot remember. But I remember it was old. And it smelled
old too. It was very big, and I was quite small so could
easily have fit my whole body in there. I imagined I would
find a Narnia of my own inside it, if I entered. Maybe I did.
Maybe I didn't. I would never tell a soul.

RUNAWAY

I was listening to the ocean
I saw a face in the sand
But when I picked it up then it vanished away from my hands
I had a dream I was seven
Climbing my way in a tree
I saw a piece of heaven waiting patient for me

And I was running far away
Would I run off the world some day?
Nobody knows, nobody knows
And I was dancing in the rain
I felt alive and I can't complain
But now take me home
Take me home where I belong
I can't take it any more

I was painting a picture
The picture was a painting of you
And for a moment I thought you were here
But then again it wasn't true
And all of this time I have been lying
Lying in secret to myself
I've been putting sorrow on the farest place on my shelf

And I was running far away
Would I run off the world some day?
Nobody knows, nobody knows
And I was dancing in the rain
I felt alive and I can't complain
But now take me home
Take me home where I belong
I got no other place to go
I can't take it any more

But I kept running for a soft place to fall
And I kept running for a soft place to fall

Take me home where I belong
I can't take it any more

RUNAWAY

This song has grown so much larger than I even believed.
It's a very strange feeling.

But it's beautiful to know something you've made,
has the ability to touch people's hearts.

I remember so clearly when I started writing it.
I was around 11 and had just come home from school.
It was February, and it was awfully cold outside.

In my childhood home, my piano sits in the living room,
right next to the window.
These windows are tall and large, and they make the wall
seem like a portal to the outside world.
It's beautiful.

Back then they were smaller, and each window was divided
into two perfect squares at the top, with two rectangular
shapes at the bottom.
It made them feel much less like a portal
and more like a prison.
Not that I felt trapped or anything, but it definitely made
the outside world seem a little further away.
And a little more out of touch.

Still, beyond the glass lies the fjord I grew up in.
The fjord of light.
The water was completely still.
And it drew me in.

I've always found silence
to be the most inspiring thing of all.
And as I looked outside, and bathed in the stillness
of my room, I felt as if I could hear the ocean.

And so, the first line of 'Runaway' begins.
Simple.
But very descriptive of the emotion I was feeling
right there and then.
It allowed me to tell a story feeling like the whole world
was listening.

Like most of my early songs, grief and death play a very
important part of the first seed of this one.
When you mourn someone, and you feel as if you see their
face everywhere.

It was not until I had just turned 15 that I added the part
about running away from your grief.
I had just experienced a loss that came so unexpectedly
and abruptly, I didn't know what to do with myself.

The grief took up so much space in me
I had to get away from it.
And I ran so far, I started missing home.
And I started missing myself.
I didn't deal with it very well.
And I wasn't kind to myself.
But I think this can be hard to do when you're only 15.

Grief must be felt.
And by doing so we honour it.
It's ok to give yourself time.
We all grieve differently.
Some people need to step back into the real world to survive,
and some people need to take a large break from it.
And this is ok.
With time it almost becomes beautiful.
Because grief changes the way you look at the world.
And yourself.
And your loved ones that are still here.

Now 'Runaway' has become something much
larger than grief.
Because all of you have given it the honour
to become comfort.
Medicine.
Peace and stillness.

It's so powerful.

oh   I am listening to the Occean
I ~~been~~ saw her face in   the sand
but   wen I picked It up then It
wanished away   from my hand.

I had a dream I was seven
climbing   my way up a tree
I looked   oupen   the heaven I
notised   a   peace   wating for me

Then I was running on the street,
I flyed away and I lost my fretl
dadida didadida didadadddaa

And   I was dancing in the rain I
felt alaive I cant complayn.
but oh, take me down , take me down
on the ground

I was painting A picture, the
picture was a painting or you, for
a moment   I thought you were
her but   then again It wont true

All this time I have been
lying. lying in secret to myself.
I've been hiding sorrow far
behind all the things on my shelf

then I was running far away, would
I run of the wourld somday.
no One knows! ~~No, no~~ I say, no one knows!

I felt it iching in my nose, in my
fingertips in my little toes.
but oh, take me home, take me
home wer I belong...
I cant take it anymore.

then I fell, like rain is falling down.
I fell like a stone Against the ground
this emptyness inside my hart has
been ther from the start

but I cept running.

please!!!

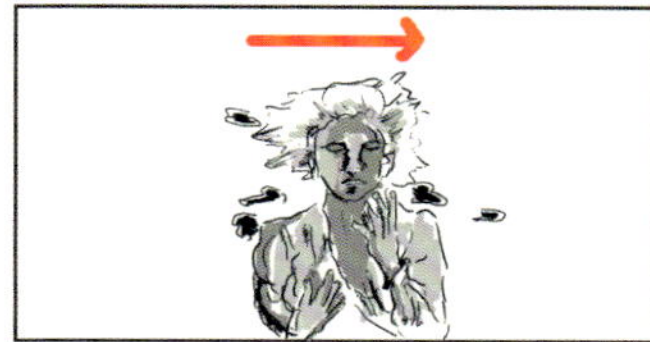

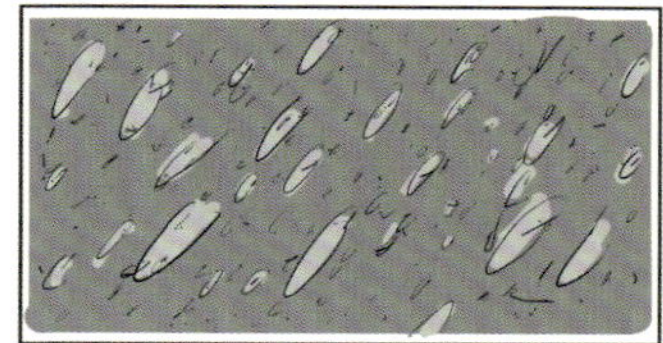

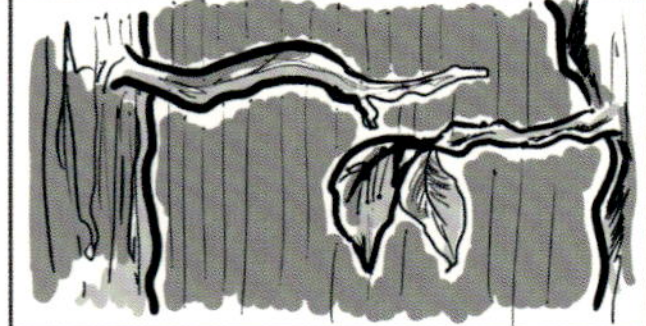

'Runaway' video storyboard by Kenny McCracken

The mirror scenes are set up somewhere in each location. We set up time lapse of these. We will see the sky passing in the mirror while the landscape will appear still or moving rapidly in the breeze. The next three slides represent the different locations we will be setting this up in.

We change the time lapse camera to the film camera and shoot in slow motion items from the surrounding enviroment, reflected in the mirrors. After this happens for a bit we intentionally smash the mirror, allowing the mirror to fall and the enviroment to take centre stage.

We catch shards of mirror falling through the air.

These shots will be shot at super high resolution so we can track in and out with ease, allowing us to visit them at many different points throught the track.

We have a tight shot of the glass hitting the ground and coming to rest in the enviroment. Most of the shards will come to rest reflecting the sky or reflecting the surrounding environment, creating a portal in the ground into a reversed world below ground level.

We establish Aurora running through one wooded location. This saves time and creates one cinematic narrative scene within the film. It will be shot with one specific outfit for Aurora to wear.

(If we find time on each location we will catch other bits of running regardless of clothes).

2:30, the track slows down and the lyric "running for a soft place to fall" comes in. At this point we see Aurora falling away from the camera. This is shot from several different angles. This establishes the original scene where she is lying down.
This is shot in slow motion and is drawn out and mixed with all the other vinyettes in the film.

We lock the camera off and let Aurora run through the scene as well as track with her front, back and from the side. This will allow us to cut rapidly, giving the feeling of drama as the track picks up.

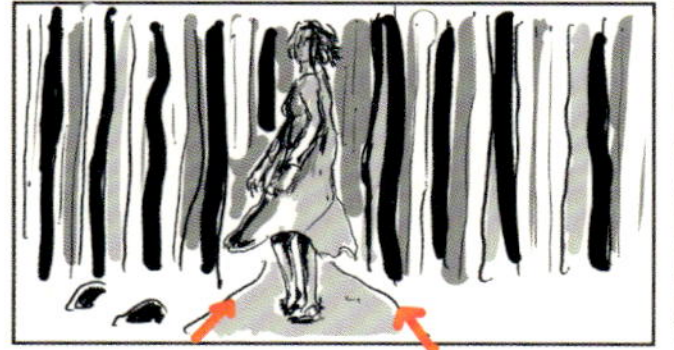

Again, we will edit in and out of this vinyette in the later sections of the track.

The final shot of the film is the lifeless body of Aurora. Just before the final cut to black, we see her eyes open.

I lost my things again.
It doesn't surprise me since I always lose everything
— I think I might quit school.
I like my teacher. And I like my friends.
But I don't feel like I can be here anymore.

This is not an ordinary day in young Aurora's life.
This is the day I learned how to swim.
I used to fear the ocean and its waves for fear of being
swallowed. And here you can see, the wave feels more like
a kiss on the back of the head. It was delicious. And I
couldn't believe that something so large and mysterious as
the ocean itself could feel like somewhere safe. It was
after my mother told me swimming feels like flying that
I really put my mind into learning how to do it.

CONQUEROR

CONQUEROR

Broken mornings, broken nights and broken days in between
Open ground, the sky is open, makes an old bird sing

Just like in fiction and every addiction
Oh, fantasy taking over, awake me

I've been looking for the conqueror
But you don't seem to come my way
I've been looking for the only one
But you don't seem to come my way

Broken me and broken them
You are broken too
Open ears, their eyes are open
Makes me call for you

But there's no seduction only destruction
Oh, fantasy take me over and break me

I've been looking for the conqueror
But you don't seem to come my way
I've been looking for the only one
But you don't seem to come my way

But I feel alive
I feel alive…

CONQUEROR

'Conqueror' was the first and last song I absolutely hated.
Listening to it now, I don't find it all that bad.
But at the time it felt like the end of the world.

I do apologise to whoever out there is offended by this.
It's ok for me if you love this song.
As long as you are ok with the lack of love
I felt for it at the time.

I didn't know how it could hurt so much to release something
I found both amusing and entertaining simply because it didn't
feel like me.
It felt too simple.
And not deep enough.

Maybe because it felt more like a butterfly than a moth.
Or maybe just because I thought it was strange and scary
to write something that sounded so happy and carefree.

I don't know.

This song honestly made me almost quit being an artist.
I had to perform it on so many television shows, and with them
a small taste of fame came into my life.
And I didn't like the fame.
It felt like such a large sacrifice that I was opening up the
doors to my sacred soul with a song that had nothing to do
with it.

Luckily, by the end of my massively busy touring year of 2016,
I spoke my truth, calm and clear.
That if I ever feel unsure about any kind of music again,
I will not release it.
And everyone understood.
And by this I learned that everyone around me are much more
willing to help me have my way than I thought.

I also learned that imperfection is fine.
But I need to feel in touch with the art that I do.
And since then, I always have.

And it's wonderful.

I produced my first album together with Magnus Skylstad and
Odd Martin Skålnes. They have both become very dear friends of
mine and making this album together is something I would never
change if I was ever given the option.

I remember knowing what I wanted.
And knowing how clear an idea I had for my music
and how I wanted it to sound.
I remember being scared to let other ideas in.
And I remember feeling overwhelmed by leaving the safe feeling
of writing on my own in my room, to suddenly being three heads
trying to collide with caution.

Luckily, I became very good at standing my ground.
And luckily, both Magnus and Odd Martin are brilliant people,
with good heads on their shoulders
and good hearts in their chests.
They offered me a lot of space to be myself.
And they pushed me, not too hard, but a bit to make sure
I allowed myself to grow.
Happily, most of the people I worked with back then
were such kind souls.
I chose them all quite carefully.

Magnus and Odd Martin. Michelle and Nico.
Electric (Henrik and Edvard). Jeremy and Alf.
All good people.
All gentle souls.
I thank you all.
I'm saying this because I want to speak to all new artists out
there who feel overwhelmed or mistreated. If you feel pushed
into the wrong direction, or made to feel like you have to
change in order to be loved by the world, you are working with
the wrong people.

Making music should be fun.
And being yourself should feel safe.

Choose kind people.
Surround yourself with people you trust.
People who care about art. And emotion. And music.
And not about all that other crap.

You are who you are for a reason, and if you were ever to
change who you are, the world would suffer a great loss.
Because there is only one of you.
And if you're not yourself, suddenly there is none of you.
And that is simply sad.

It's normal to be overwhelmed in the beginning.
It's normal to feel like you're losing yourself.
Because there will be a lot of people that have a lot to say
about you and your music.

But you know the best.
And you should never forget that.

I learnt so much from my first album.
I learnt that a song can't be completely ruined even if you
don't love the sound of your snare and you don't have time
to fix it.
As long as the soul of the song is clear.
That will be what people notice the most.

And I learnt to never put a song on any album
where the soul is unclear.
Follow your gut.
The gut is a fantastic brain.
And it should NOT be ignored.

Magnus, Odd Martin and I travelled so much. The three of us. It meant the world to me to travel the world with people I loved. I think this is one of our first visits to the BBC. I can't remember how it was to be there, or at all what we did. But I remember we had much fun afterwards. We had no idea how much was about to happen.

Transmission
Mic Live
MIC LIVE
PRES 1 2 3 4 5 6 7 8
TBU 1 TBU 2
TBU 3 TBU 4
TX ACTIVE
TX A
TX B
OS 1 – News
OS 2– Weather
OS 3– Big Q
OS 4–PARK HD
OS 7–R2 DAB
OS 8–PARK HD
OS 9–PARK HD
OS 10–PARK HD
PREVIEW
Cam 1
Cam 2
Cam 3
Cam 4
CHEER UP
GATE
PFL
Current Assignment
CAJUN IN
PRESETS
Current Assignment
CAJUN IN
PRESETS
EQ
Dynamics 1
Gain Reduction
Reset EQ A
Reset EQ B
Compressor /
Limiter Meter
ON
Copy EQ Settings

CAMERA 3
TX C
TX D
marr
The Andrew Marr Show
OS 5–PARK HD
OS 6–PARK HD
OS 11–Edit LK OP
OS 12–Edit LL OP
BLANKED
PROMPT
Cam 6
Snoop Cam 1
ITOR DESK 1 FOR WORLD & DESK 2 FOR NATIONALS
LAYER 2   Gp1: OS's   Gp2: Mics   Gp3: Reps   Gp4: S'by Mics
ARTEMIS
MTR1
Main 1 Line
Main 2 Line
Main 3 Line
Main 4 Line
Main 5 Line
Main 6 Line
Main 7 Line
Main 8 Line
Current Assignment
428
Layer 1
PRESETS
EQ
Dynamics 1
WARNING

"Conqueror"

the boy is a character
i've been inspired by
for a long time.

"little boy in the grass"

a haunted boy.

He's stuck in his own
bubble. parted from
the rest of the world.

I need to reach out to
him.
do i need to save him?
or do i need him
to save me?

we were poor.
before we put our
feet into the mud.

we cant hear
our mothers calling
us back home

we were clean
before they ~~told us~~ tought
~~about~~ us ~~hotel~~ how to
run against our dreams

or so it seems

Running with the Wolves

Go row the boat to safer grounds
But don't you know
We're stronger now
My heart still beats
And my skin still feels
My lungs still breathe
My mind still feels

But we're running out of time
All the echoes in my mind, cry

There's blood on your lies
The scars open wide
There is nowhere for you to hide,
The hunter's moon is shining

I'm running with the wolves tonight
I'm running with the wolves
I'm running with the…

Trick or treat
What would it be?
I walk alone
I'm everything
My ears can hear
And my mouth can speak
My spirit talks
I know my soul believes

But we're running out of time
All the echoes in my mind, cry

I'm running with the wolves tonight
I'm running with the wolves

A gift, a curse
They track and hurt
Say can you dream in nightmare, seems
A million voices silent screams
Where hope is left so incomplete

I'm running with the wolves

I'm running with the wolves tonight
I'm running with the wolves

People always told me that I had so much sadness in my eyes.
But sadness isn't always a bad thing.
It has so many different forms and reasons.
Sometimes something is so beautiful it almost makes me sad to
think about them. Sometimes it's simply because I am touched.
Sometimes I don't even know why it's there.
But I do know that I always welcome it, this temporary guest.
You should always treat a guest with kindness.

Something I didn't think about much when I was a child,
but I've learned to appreciate later, is that when I was
little my parents never thought I was strange. When the
world called me so, they always answered with, "Well, she
is a child. It's their job to be a little strange".

And I can't help but mention how much that
might have helped me through the years.
It's helped me simply exist.
And to all parents with children who they fear might
be bullied, never let your fear for them intervene
with the love you have for them.

We all learn with time.
Sadly, we also learn to fit in, and some brilliant
attributes might be lost in the process of it all.

Tell them to be.
Encourage their imagination.

Their need to dress as strangely as they want.
Support their need to be alone sometimes.

Teach them that bullies simply bully because they
are judgemental and not curious.

Children should be curious.
And strange.
And free.
As long as they are allowed to be.

And whatever we turn out to be as adults is ok.
Because at least we are ourselves.
And strong individuals have always been, and will
always be, a very important thing in this world.

Much love to all strange kids out there x

LUCKY

When I am down
I lay my hands upon this ground
For the thousandth time
I call him in, his earth is mine

Before I make the offering
Remember all the faces that I've seen
The marks have settled on my skin
From all the different places that I've been
That I've been

And I feel the light for the very first time
Not anybody knows that I am lucky to be alive

War inside my mind behind my eyes
It's coming down
For the thousandth time
I feel too numb to even mind

Before I make the offering
Remember all the faces that I've seen
Now all the marks have settled on my skin
From all the different places that I've been
That I've been

And I feel the light for the very first time
Not anybody knows that I am lucky to be alive

I don't know where I am, or where I'll go
Where to even begin when I know
What lies behind makes no sense in my mind
But I know that it's time to let go

I dont feel like myself
anymore.

What is there to say

WINTER BIRD

Walking in my sleep
Like the naked dreams
Will they wake up again?
Do they sleep, do they dream?

Feel it as the wind
Strokes my skin
I am moved by the chill
Hear the winter bird sing

My tears are always frozen, I can see the air I breathe
Got my fingers painting pictures on the glass in front of me
Lay me by the frozen river where the boats have passed me by
All I need is to remember how it was to feel alive

Silent days, violent shades
We are dancing again in a dream by the lake

My tears are always frozen, I can see the air I breathe
Got my fingers painting pictures on the glass in front of me
Lay me by the frozen river where the boats have passed me by
All I need is to remember how it was to feel alive

Rest against my pillow like the ageing winter sun
Only wake each morning to remember that you're gone
So I drift away again to Winter I belong

My tears are always frozen, I can see the air I breathe
Got my fingers painting pictures on the glass in front of me
Lay me by the frozen river where the boats have passed me by
All I need is to remember how it was to feel alive

I need to remember how it was to feel alive

The raven is my favourite bird.

Not so surprisingly, this is another animal
that is known to represent death.
But the raven also represents wisdom and prophecy.

In some ways it represents transformation too.
Like all things that represent death.
Death can mean so much more than we think.

I used to know a raven.
As much as it would let me.
It's the one that I have drawn
in one of my ancient books written by my past self.

I always imagined the raven would come visit me
to tell me something.
As either a warning or a sign that something
grand and beautiful was about to happen.
Odin had two ravens.
And they gifted him with information about
the world — according to Norse mythology.

I only had one.
And whatever it was that he gifted me was
very much up to me to decipher on my own.

I still don't quite know.
But it always lifted my mood when I saw him resting his
wings on one of the branches of the tree outside my window.

I named him Edna.
And at this very moment I don't have the patience
to explain to you why.
This is my gift to you.

A riddle of no importance to chew on.

I remember this was the most like myself I had
ever felt in a piece of clothing. I felt like
a bird dressed in its own ashes. This made this
particular day into a very good one. Bless the
birds. And bless the ashes.

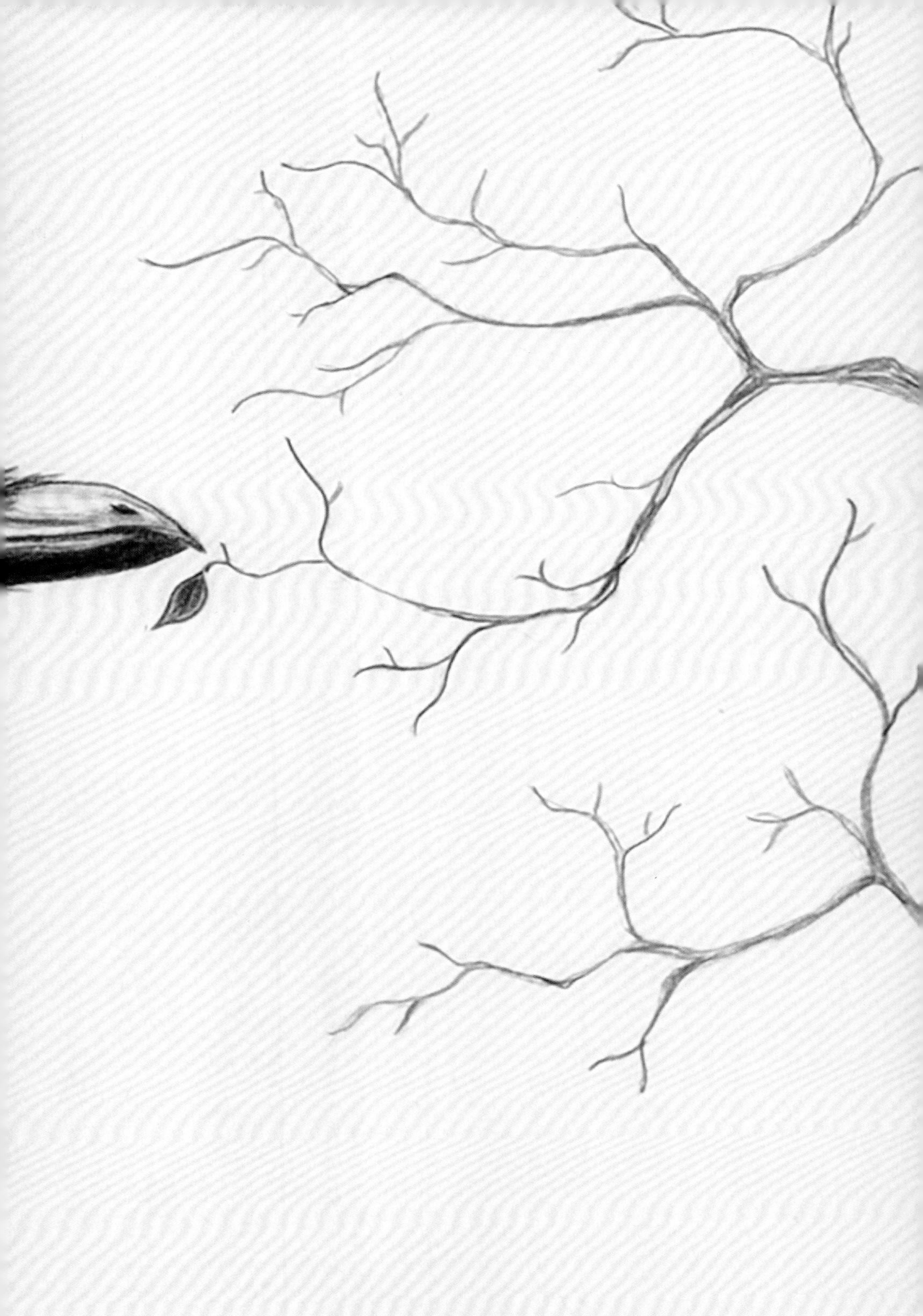

I WENT TOO FAR

I went too far when I was begging on my knees
Begging for your arms, for you to hold around me
I went too far and kissed the ground beneath your feet
Waiting for your love, waiting for our eyes to meet

Crying, give me some love!
Give me some love and hold me
Give me some love and hold me tight

I went too far when I was begging on my knees
When I cut my hands so you could stand and watch me bleed
I went too far and kissed the ground beneath your feet
Standing in my blood it was the taste of bittersweet

Crying, give me some love!
Give me some love and hold me
Give me some love and hold me tight

Why can't I turn around and walk away
Go back in time?
I had to turn around and walk away
I couldn't stay, I had to walk away

I'm left behind with an empty hole
And everything I am is gone
I try to reach for another soul
So I can feel whole

I am so happy I signed to Decca all those years ago.
Decca asked me about who I was and what I wanted to say.
They never spoke about money, or greatness, simply —
what do I, as an artist dream about? That is when I knew
they were right for me. Because they were like me — curious.

Here you see a picture of me and my friend Benedict who works
at Decca (now called Fontana). He is a brilliant soul.
And I feel so forever grateful.

Right now, Benedict and his wonderful partner Kayla
are some of my best friends.
And I feel so completely honoured by knowing someone like this.
Completely unique.

The reason why I am writing about this is: to all new
artists out there — your greatness is already in you.

Find people you could imagine being friends with,
and you will always achieve what is most important —
to blossom as the human you are.

Nothing more or less.
Just you.

The world needs individuals who are comfortable in
their own skin, so we can all learn how to be the same.
And being yourself, truly, is so much easier when
you are surrounded by friends.

Working should be fun,
it should not make you sad or stressed,
it should make you laugh, and dance.
And from these life experiences, music comes.

Like a river out of your soul.

I don't know
much abot love.

WARRIORS AND WEIRDOS
____

I remember very well how I came up with the name
for our fandom.
Of our community.
Or whatever you want to call it.

I was asked about it so many times, and at first I didn't
understand what people meant.
We already have names so why do we need another one?
But then I guess I noticed what a beautiful thing it is,
when people gather together in these safe spaces
music makes for us.

And names are powerful.

So of course, I had to find a name for the people
that gather in the safe space my music creates.
Or even more so, the safe space the people
around my music create.
All of you.

I remember being uncomfortable with the name having to do
too much with my name.
Because in my mind the people that admired my music
weren't mine.
They belonged to themselves.

It was my music that was theirs, or yours.
And then I used my eyes and looked at the very people
that tended to gravitate towards me and to my delight,
I discovered that many of you were a lot like me.
And it made me feel so understood.

You are all really, really strange people.
Interesting people.
Complicated people.

So, I wanted to find something grand that explained us.

At first.

WEIRDOS.

It felt cute. And I liked the way the W looks.
I also like many words that begin with this letter.
Words like Wizard. Or Whimsical. Warm or Willing. Whimsy.
Willow. Wish. Worthy. Wise. Wholesome. Wonderful. Wonder.
Wonderous. Wander. Whole. Wild. And so many more.

But I also felt a unique goodness from the people who
listened to my music.
A kindness that is rare when a group grows large.
A kindness and empathy that comes from people who know what
it feels like to battle.
This made me settle for one more name.

WARRIOR.

Because weird people know how it is to be outcasts.
How it is to fight a little more to be understood
and loved and accepted for who they are.
Especially back then.

People who are weird are often automatically warriors too,
because of the courage it requires to simply exist.

Of course, I know this phenomenon exists
far beyond our community.
And far beyond the world of my music.

I think we all feel misunderstood and peculiar.
Some people are just better at hiding it.
But that doesn't mean it doesn't weigh on their shoulders.
One simply can never know from just looking at someone.

WARRIORS AND WEIRDOS.
There it is.

Cute.

FPS 25.000   SHUTTER 180.0
SDI
LOOK
CAM
3.2K
LOG C
BAT 13.4V
A 003   C003

EI 400   ND -   WB   2800 K   +0.0 C
WARRIOR
DIR: FRACTION
CAM: WRIGHT
SCENE
SLATE
TAKE
A003
2
1
DATE: 10/03/16
PANAVISION

WARRIOR

I fall asleep in my own tears
I cry for the world for everyone
And I build a boat to float in
I'm floating away

I can't recall the last time I opened my eyes to see the world as beautiful
And I built a cage to hide in
I'm hiding, I'm trying to battle the night

Let love conquer your mind
Warrior, Warrior
Just reach out for the light
Warrior, Warrior
I am Warrior
Warrior, Warrior
I am Warrior
Warrior of love

I stand behind a wall of people and thoughts, mind controlling
And I hold a sword to guide me, I'm fighting my way

I can't recall the last time I opened my eyes to see the world as beautiful
And I built a cage to hide in
I'm hiding, I'm trying to battle the night

Underneath darkened skies
There's a light that don't lie

Let love conquer your mind
Warrior, Warrior
Just reach out for the light
Warrior, Warrior
I am Warrior
Warrior, Warrior
I am Warrior
Warrior of love

Troubadour

Blanchard pinx.

1. *Sphinx tête de mort*. (Acherontia atropos, Lin.) _ 2. *Zygène de*

Fournier sculp.

endule .(Zygæna filipendulæ, Lin.) _ 3 . *Syntomide phegée* .(Syntomis phegea.Lin.)

When I was six, I travelled outside of Norway for the first
time. I only knew a tiny bit of English and I was quite
concerned about it. Communication is so important, and
I strongly dislike when it's jeopardised. But then again,
we always have music.

I knew I could find a way to thank the people who touched
my soul, knowing I would never see them again. Not because
I particularly liked singing in front of others, I didn't
really like that at all. But sometimes a little discomfort
is worth the magic created between two people as they meet
for the first and last time. This is a waiter from Greece
whose name I can't remember, but I remember him really well.

I felt like he was a very kind man. And he noticed
I didn't like when the sauce touched the food.
I liked him.

He was the first person I ever sang to. In his ear, after
eating. So I could (without words) say that it meant
something to me.

And it was wonderful.

THROUGH THE EYES OF A CHILD

The world is covered by our trails
Scars we cover up with pain
Watch them breach in sour lies
I would rather see the world through the eyes of a child
Through the eyes of a child

Darker times will come and go
Times you need to see her smile
And mothers' hearts are warm and mild
I would rather feel this world through the skin of a child
Through the skin of a child

When a human strokes your skin
That is when you let them in
Let them in before they go
I would rather feel alive with a childlike soul
With a childlike soul

Please don't leave me here

This song has changed for me during the years.
It's very magical to me, to see how a song can shapeshift
and become whatever you need it to be in the moment.
Even if you've heard it a million times.

When I wrote it, I thought about the inner child.
How the child in us would always speak up
if they saw anything unfair.
How they would always choose to be curious
instead of judgemental.
How they would see a friend in a stranger,
and magic in the most ordinary things.
A child hears music and dances.
A child trusts the people around them.
Remaining childlike keeps us all so in touch with the very
thing that makes us good people.
Playful people. Imaginative people.

I could talk about this for hours, but I'm currently writing
this little segment on my phone in my bed in Chile and my
arms are starting to ache.

(Anyways) the inner child is important.
And this song was a dedication to it.

And a wish to never lose these abilities
when the world is overwhelmingly disappointing.
Now, almost 10 years later I feel this song more than ever.

When I perform this song, I can see that you do too.

And it moves me in a strange way, that right now
the world is really testing us.
Who are we as people when we see something unfair happening?
How do we react to something we don't understand?
How welcoming can we be towards strangers?
How much magic are we capable of finding
in the most ordinary things?

Do we remember to dance when we hear music?
Do we remember to put our trust in people?
Do we remember to play?

It's fascinating.
Because it's something you have to hold onto so dearly.
And it's something you have to remember every day
until it once again becomes a part of our nature.

darker
~~troubled~~ times will come and go
whispering to the troubled mi~~
times you need to see her smi~~
mother hands are warm and mil~~

I would rather ~~feel~~ the wour~~
~~through~~ the ~~eyes~~ of a child
skin

when a human strokes your skin. open up
and let them in
let them in before they go
I would rather feel the world with a
song in my soul

2:29
door is open. eyes are closed
I remember in my mind how I hea~~
my body go from ~~the~~ corner of theroo~~
to the corner of my bed
with a song in my ear and a dea~~
inside my head
I would rather feel the world thry th~~

the world is covered by our trails

(1) hear them preach in sour
    (watch)
rain

l

I was born with open eyes

eyes

1:50 hands are little men. they are strong
and they know how to carry me home
every word is undone every leaf
in onward
I would rather feel the world
as a wind or a song?

a child

3:09 born morning

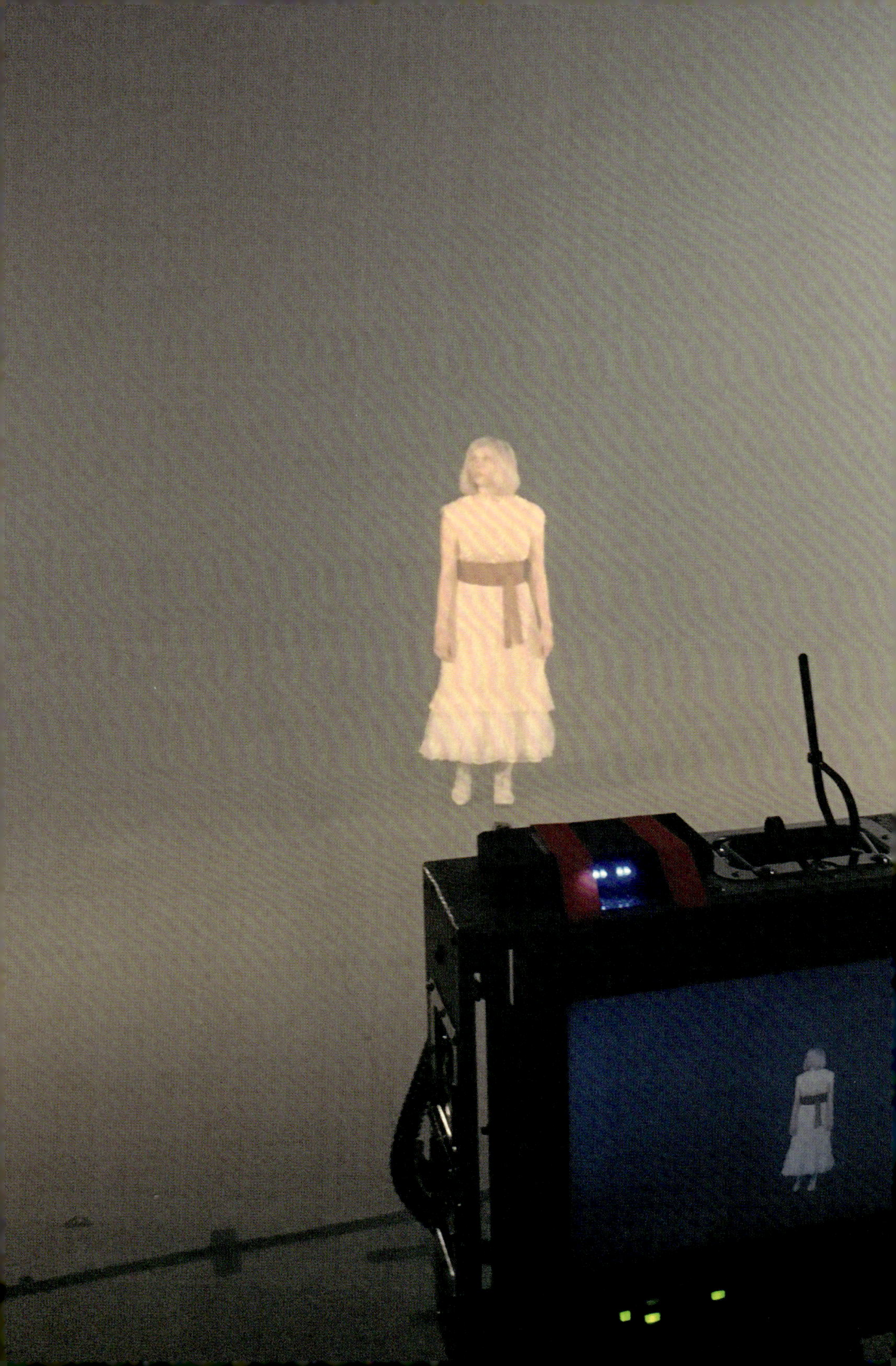

MURDER SONG (5,4,3,2,1)

5, 4, 3, 2, 1
5, 4, 3, 2, 1

He holds the gun against my head
I close my eyes, and bang I am dead
I know he knows that he's killing me for mercy
And here I go

He holds my body in his arms
He didn't mean to do no harm
And he holds me tight
He did it all to spare me from the awful things in life that come
And he cries and cries

I know he knows that he's killing me for mercy
And here I go

He holds my body in his arms
He didn't mean to do no harm
And he cries and cries
He did it all to spare me from the awful things in life that come
And he cries and cries

5, 4, 3, 2, 1
5, 4, 3, 2, 1

The gun is gone
And so am I
And here I go

MURDER SONG

I don't know why, but I wrote so much about death
when I was a child.
It feels too insensitive to simply imply
that I was fascinated by it.
And therefore, I wrote so much about it.
But that is the case.
Death is so unavoidable.
And it's so common in this world.

Some cultures see it as the end.
But others see death as just another transformation.
Death might not be an end, but a continuation
that allows us to exist somewhere else.
As something or someone else.

I wish we spoke about death more.
I wish we learnt how to mourn more openly.

I don't know if this was something I was trying to do
whenever I wrote about death.
But it felt good to touch on it.
Because death is a part of life.
And it should be honoured and spoken about
as much as everything else.

Some people die peacefully.
Whilst others violently.

And in 'Murder Song' I wanted to write about the latter.
I didn't often put my own stories into songs,
because there was so much on earth I wanted to address first.
Many of my songs are stories that aren't my own.
But they still feel very close to my heart.
'Murder Song' is one of those stories.
And it's a story you see come to life all too often
in our world.

Each time I sing it I think about them.
All those women around the world, killed by the people
who were supposed to love and protect them.
For all of you who have ever been close to such danger.
Such anger.
It's a song I will never stop singing.

respect.

a carpet lying
~~cold~~ white bricks on the floor
covered ~~each~~ ch~~

pictures bearing ~~ the ~~
~~cover~~

5 4 3 2 1.

you hold, the gun
against my head

8 ~~~~, I close my eyes

but that was yet so
~~and other~~ long ago
when he was just a litt
boy
with open eyes and with
a soul ready to live
and then with time he
realized
it's been a while now
since he smiled
and he grew bitter as
the world forgot his nam
and now he lives in
there alone
inside the fear he calls
his home
and every memorie is gon
~~toge~~ along with friends
and company
there is no joy here lef
~~for~~ me to reap
he shuts his eyes and
falls asleep, his mind is
floating in the deep

THE BITTER MAN

he thinks like only bitter
man can.

he was just a little man
and he walked his ways
alone
he ~~forgot~~ to remembered
all his seeds
but forgot to let them
grow
hes afraid of butterflies
of bicycles and all the
eyes of other people walking
by
hes afrad of going out
he likes to stay inside
his house
he was forgotten long ago
he is alone
but he remember that
one time the pretty ~~woman~~
girl
gave him a smile
and made him happy
for a while
he felt warm
where memories can keep you warm ♡

Norway

@ little bike

HOME

Lost in the moment again
Stuck where the road has no end
Keeping the thought in our minds
One day life will be kind

We are not alive
We are surviving every time
We are not alive
Only dreams inside our minds

We are home

Endless days of complaint
Forcing the light to our veins
Keeping the hope in our minds
One day life will be kind

Wrapped inside a cocoon made of flesh and bones
Doesn't really matter where you come from
We are home

Calm again
I feel warm again
I'm reborn again
I am warm inside, for a little while
I'm fine?

lost in the moment again
 stuck where the road has
no end.
keeping the thought in
our minds..
.. one day life will be
kind.

we are not alive.
we are surviving every time
we are not alive
only dreams inside our minds

we are home.

endless days of complains
forcing the light throug
our veins
keeping the hope in our
minds
one day life will be kind

HOME

I have known people to fall into the arms of substance abuse
during this life.
And one thing I know is that they were always good people.

It's strange how this world forgets
about the people who need help.
Who live amongst us, on a frequency
we often don't even notice.

I wrote this song called 'Home' about the people
who the world forgot about.
Who tried to forget themselves, who they are,
where they came from and how life has treated them.
When life offers us no dreams, and no shelter. No aid or
support. I fear our bodies begin to feel like a vessel.
A prison for your soul.
And so we do the only thing we can, we flee.

Keeping the hope in our minds
"One day life will be kind".

UNDER THE WATER

Under the water we can't breathe, we can't breathe
Under the water we die
Under the water there is no one watching
Under the water we are alone

Then why do we jump in?
Why do we jump in?
Under the water we die

So many souls that lost control
Where do they fall?
Into the deep, what do they seek
Where do they fall?

Hearts will dream again
Lungs will breathe in
Wash away the sins
It's where they begin
Fear won't fail you now
Arms won't let you down
Wash away the sins
It's where we begin

Under the water we can't be together
Under the water we die
Then why do we jump in?
Why do we jump in?
Under the water we die

I love heavy metal.
It has played a very big part in my youth.
There is something about being attacked by a wall of sound
that is so aggressively comforting.
This song was my little way of honouring a world that has
brought me so much joy.

Also...
It is surprisingly hard to sing well whilst headbanging.
I don't know how they do it.

let me swallow
your mind
you are beautiful.

Tired but happy.

2016 was my first touring year and I don't think I've
toured that much ever since. It was unbelievably busy.
And I have promised myself to never do that again.

Now I know how to tour and take care of myself.
This makes me feel like I could do it forever.

This photo reminds me that I didn't always know that.
And I can see it.
It makes me both sad and happy.
Because I know now, with time, things got better.

BIRTH SCREAMS

I was born screaming
but i feel I will die
in silence.

Birth screams
an crying
like I knew what
was coming my way

Birth sscreams

I dont remember
the first time eyes opened

but i ~~tell~~ feel the same
thing happens every
morning

BLACK WATER LILIES

When I am on a boat
I float, I know I can never drown
I see underwater land
The wind is the only sound

Take your hand and I go under
I'm under and above
Take your hand and I go under
I'm under and above

On the river I'm floating in
On the water I'm diving in
To the ocean a thousand black water lilies
In the river I'm floating in
Under water I'm diving into the ocean,
A thousand black water lilies

Arms are reaching for my arms I can see no more
We dance as we float around
We head towards the ocean floor

Take your hand and I go under
I'm under and above

On the river I'm floating in
On the water I'm diving in
To the ocean a thousand black water lilies
In the river I'm floating in
Under water I'm diving into the ocean
A thousand black water lilies

I am born
Falling out
I am reborn

Water lilies, water lilies, water lilies

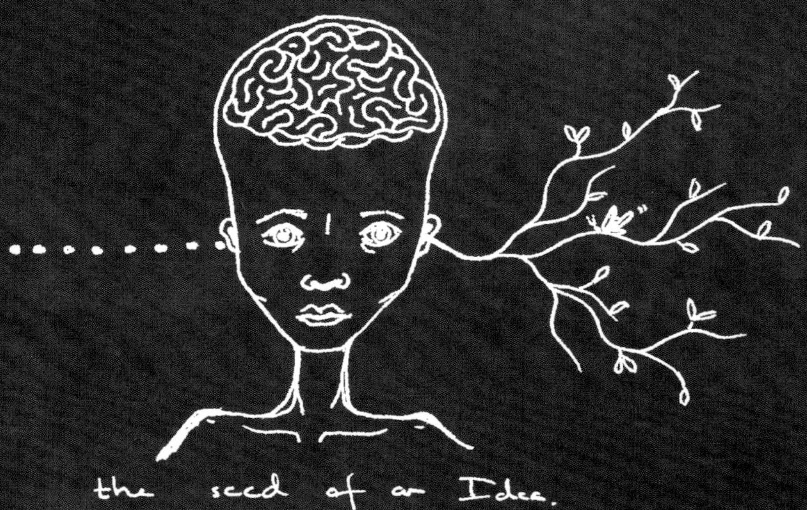
the seed of an Idea.

BLACK WATER LILIES
____

This was the most fun song to produce.
We searched for sounds so freely.
It felt like hunting.
Like instinct.
Simply marvellous.

I would kiss you.

if I could.

but your not
mine to kiss
on an airport
in amsterdam.

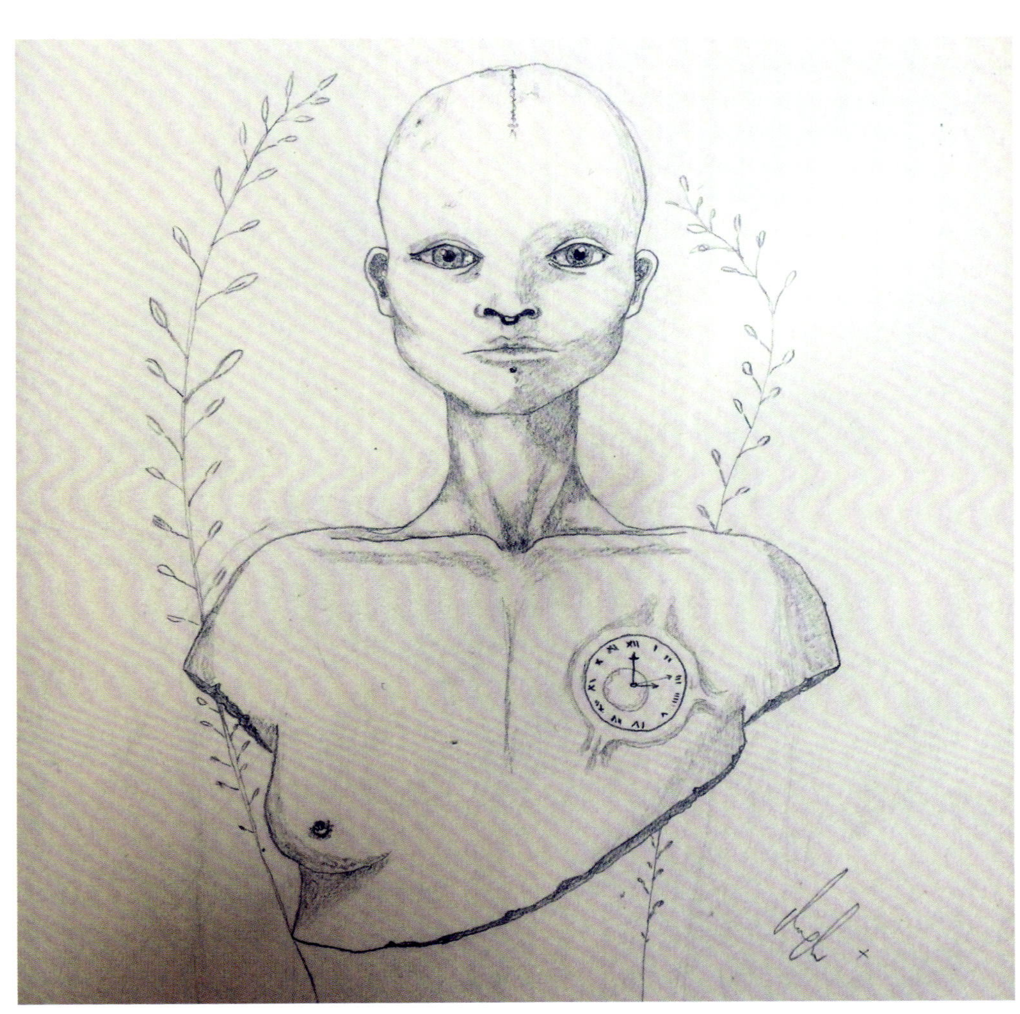

WISDOM CRIES

We go way back in time through diamond eyes…
We go way back in time through diamond eyes…

We gotta go back to the start, back to…
We are back home
We gotta go back to the start, back to…
We are back home

[Tick tock, tick tock]

Where is the light?
Are we meant to go down again?

Lightning strikes
Wisdom cries emergency, emergency
Conscious all night
No one's surprised
As long as we
Emergency, emergency

Wisdom cries
Wisdom cries

WISDOM CRIES
____

'Wisdom Cries' is the last song of my first chapter.
To me the last song on an album always feels like the
portal that goes into the next one.

I remember recording in Germany.
Me and Michelle and Nico were harvesting something
really strange whilst recording this.
Something both the raven and the moth would approve of.

It felt very important to me at the time
to have it on the album.
A song that made sense while also making no sense at all.

The title still touches me.

Can you believe how long humans have existed on this earth?
And that despite all warnings or lessons learnt the
hard way, we still manage to forget all the things we
are supposed to have learnt.

The world I see before me now is truly as horrendous
as it is beautiful.

Just like us.

I repeatedly have to remind myself that as long as I do
what I can to level out the bad that I see, knowing so many
people try to do the same, the world will be fine.
It won't be perfect. But it will be fine.
And besides, we already came to terms with the fact that
perfection isn't important.
The soul is.

And music is such the language of the soul.
We all speak it fluently.

BERLIN

PI
—

I keep finding these random numbers of Pi
between the pages of my poetry.
I can't remember when I stopped doing it.
But I know back then, it used to make me feel calm.
Actually, it still does.

3,14159265 3589793238 46264

3383279502 884 1971693993

75105 82097 4944 59 230

781 6406286 208998 62803482

534211 706798 214808 651328

230664709 384460955048

223172535 9408128481 11

7450 284102701938521 11

0555 9644 6229 48954

9303819644288 1097 5665

9 33 4461 284 75648 2333

786 783 1652712 0190914564

85 6 9 234 603486 104543

266482 133 93607 602 49141

1237 245 8700660631 59881

7488 15 2092096 28 2925409

1715 36436789 259036001133

I don't remember what this was or where this even is.
But... God, how often I was surrounded by only men. The world
has changed a lot since I started out, and this makes me
so happy. There are so many more women who are absolutely
brilliant who help make this industry a better world to live in.
Amongst many men of course, some of them I have worked with
for many, many years.

People who believe in equality. In respect.
In sensitivity.
In emotions.

People who see the person, not the gender. And who wait to
judge who you are after you've had a chance to prove yourself.
Lovely.

I feel so calm.

I feel in love, yet
I know that I'm not.

I'm just happy.

Like a calm lake.

I feel so calm.

HUG x

THOUGTS

the sky is red today.
                its beautiful.
the train is moving fast only
showinrogn me glimpse of it
in between the trees and
buildings.

I like london more when I'm
on a train.

an old man is sitting on
the othe side. his hair is white
and his eyes are kind.

I tell him to look at the sky
to remember how beautiful it
is.
the man tells me tomoriow
will be a good day.
                I believe him

UNDER STARS

Mad world beats outside our hearts
Times of need, we are apart
Under stars, we are alone

Under stars

Knuckles move under his skin
He wraps his heart and drags it in
And they move it all around
Until we cry

Under stars

Mother cries and turns around
Walks outside without a sound
The rain against her skin
While she faces every sin

Under stars

They have only fallen asleep
They have only fallen asleep

I've seen it many times
Each time they close their eyes, say goodbye
Rest in peace and give yourself to harmony
Give yourself to harmony underneath the stars

washed away .. by the rain
no remains . I'm gone again

THE VIKTOR WYND
MUSEUM OF CURIOSITIES
FINE ART & NATURAL HISTORY
THE LAST TUESDAY SOCIETY

This is a photo from our first time on Conan O'Brien's TV show.
I remember I liked the moon.
I remember I liked that he had red hair.

And I remember my belt pack fell off during the song
and I had to sing without hearing anything.
It was marvellous.
Because it became so alive the minute it all went wrong.
Lovely.

OAKLAND RAIN

PUPPET

A dancing puppet doll, made of wood
I bet he'd run away one day
If he could choose to leave or stay
He's got a string attached to every bone
She's got him round her little finger
So she'll never feel alone

Oh, sometimes I wonder, did he go
But not a man, of course his soul
Dreaming about wonderland
Wakes up and he's a man

Oh, she's taking control over another man's mind
Oh, taking control over his mind

The idea of leaving her has struck his mind
When he sees her smile he's hypnotised
And he can't leave her behind
Looking to his left, there's the door
No need to try, tried it once before
And their bones hiding beneath the floor

Sometimes I wonder, did he go
But not a man, of course his soul
Dreaming about wonderland
Wakes up and he's a man

Oh, she's taking control over another man's mind
Oh, taking control over his mind

When they were out to buy her wedding gown
She wanted nothing but the dress
Over a hundred thousand pounds
But what she wants she gets, or she will cry
Hits the man with her umbrella
She'll continue till he dies

Sometimes I wonder, did he go
But not a man, of course his soul
Dreaming about wonderland
Wakes up and he's a man

Oh, taking control over another man's mind
Taking control over his mind

Puppet

A dancing doll made of wood
I'll bet he'll run away one day
if he could chose to leave or stay

he got a string attached to
every bone, she's got him round
her little finger so she'll never feel alone

Sometimes I wonder did it go?
well not the man of course, his sole
dreaming about wonderland, wake up
and be her man

"taking control over another mans mind" x2

the idea of leaving her, has struck his mind
but when he sees her smile, her hypnotize
and cant leave her behind

looking to his left, there is the door
no need to try, he tried it once before
theres numbs hiding beneath the floor

Someti
taking cont

mellowspill istedet for ret.

when they wen out to get her
wedding gown , she wanted nothing
but the dress ove a hundef f nousand
punds

what she wants she gets , or she
will cry
hits he man with his umbrella
shell continue till he dies

*
sometimes I wonder did it go? well not
the man of cuvnr his soule ←)v!!

ref

taking control ova anotha mans mind x2

mhh.—
asting the permission to walk
permission to talk
mellomspill

mh.... flos stemt.

I HAD A DREAM

Last night I had a dream that we were fighting
'Cause we had different ways in wrong rhyme
And as the words ran out and you were shouting
I saw there would be no peace in here tonight

Then I dreamt we both lost in the end
Well, you proved your point but now you have lost a friend
The light we used to live has reached the end
And we both want to smile back, though I pretend
Oh I pretend

Ah, oh I had a dream
I had a dream
But it all just seemed so real

But it all seems to be longing for this glory
To get fame and fortune of our own
But will we, in the end, be satisfied
When we're living in our glory, all alone?

And this night I had a dream that we were running
Running far away from our mistakes
We were blaming others for the wrongs we made
And then we were down because we were not the one we paid

Ah, oh I had a dream
I had a dream
Oh, I had this dream
But it all just seemed so real

One night I had a dream a man hit his woman
'Cause she was standing in the way and he was drunk
And every Monday morning she was brave
When the man drove far away inside his truck

But tonight I had a dream that we were just watching
All devastating things this world can bear
We could feel the lightness way over here
But when it didn't us concern, we didn't care

No we wouldn't lift a finger for the lost ones
We wouldn't give money to the poor
Our happiness has come in shape of gold
And we forget what's truly worth living for

Ah, I had a dream
I had a dream
Oh, I had this dream
But it all just seemed so real
It seemed so real
Just seemed so real
It seemed so real

I have these dreams and they seem so real
And they seem so much more to me than just dreams

I still long for those first shows,
simply because the audience was so near.
You could see every single soul in the room, as a constant
reminder of who you are pouring your art into.

Being so close to the audience helped me overcome my stage fright.
Because I saw them close their eyes, and cry, and smile,
while I realised — this isn't really about me, it's about them.

And so I learned to feel more like a vessel than an animal in a zoo.

I learned that a performance is something we do together,
me and the audience.

And it became less important that the talent was perfect
and more important that every show felt like natural and
real human behaviour.

Thank you to all of you that attended my first shows. Including
this one at Ace Hotel in London many million centuries ago.

AWAKENING

With a tiny rope and a bag of stones
And all her broken wishing bones
She's going in, she's going home
Oh, this little golden eye
Fighting every day
Behind the light, behind the light

Walking faster down the street
Red eyes and no shoes on her feet
Going on this journey, determined to complete
This is farewell, this is goodnight
The last time she will see the daylight
See the daylight

And she's going on a journey
Always walking down the road
And the water is always calling
'My little child, please come home'

That's when she went away
Away from the light of day

Standing by the riverside
Patiently waiting for the tide
To come along, to come along
The water's going to her feet
And on her body, wind so cold and sweet
So cold and sweet

And she's going on a journey
Always walking down the road
And the water is always calling
'My little child, please come home'
And the stars were brightly shining
When she reached out they were gone
And the water started calling
'My little child, please come home'

Feel the water in her body
Water's never going out

And she's going on a journey
Always walking down the road
And the water is always calling
'My little child, please come home'
And the stars were brightly shining
When she reached out they were gone
And the water started calling
'My little child, please come home'

When a shiny light hit her eye
And she turned around and climbed towards the sky
Towards the sky

Though the life music has brought to me has
been chaotic at times, I am still very grateful.
I am an introvert after all.
And it's hard for us when the world becomes
too large and the people too many.

There is one really good thing time has given me –
room to process it all.
And fall in love with the things that used to frighten me.
Like we all have to.
Eventually.
To cope with the paths we've chosen.

'All My Demons Greeting Me as a Friend'
was the beginning of it all.
And together with its sisters it has taken me
to where I am today.

I feel very grateful.

And I enjoyed looking into the past for a little while,
patching this book together into something
that might make sense for you all.

I know it's a bit all over the place, my thoughts, my words.
But I am a bit all over the place.
And I was even more so 10 years ago.
I didn't want to overthink my words either.
Because it would make them come from the brain
and not from the heart,
and that wouldn't be right.

Thank you to everyone who believed in me then,
you know who you are.

I wouldn't be here without you.

Much love,

AURORA

Geir, Per, Magnus, Odd Martin, Silja, Alf, Pi, Helga, Espen,
Michelle, Nico, Benjamin, Seth, Yasmine, Nadine, Olly,
Tom W, Steve, Thomas, Kim, Rudolph, Danny, Tom L, Chris,
Benedict, Fran, Holli, Laura, Dickon, Daniel, Lauren, Ed,
Ryan, Alex, Paul S.

Thank you to MADE, to BUDDE, to Petroleum, to Decca,
to Glassnote, UTA, Wasserman and Standing Ovation.

Thank you to Viktoria and Miranda who inspired so many
of my songs to come to life.
And Mama and Papa, who always supported me just like I am.

There are probably so many more.
So many people I work with now who have changed my life for
the better.
But that is for the next book.
Yes.

It's for the next book.

Last but not least;

I want to give thanks to Ken, who was my teacher at school
and told me to record my music in a real studio.
Because of you I dare to sing in front of others.
And I dared to preserve my art, by recording it, and producing it.

I wouldn't even have thought of it, since my plan was to be
a physicist.

But here I am.
I am glad I took this path.

I'm glad I found a world of my own.
And that so many of you have taken part in it.

Hugs and kisses — and, for those who understand,
(secret penises) for you all.

A

YOUR PATIENCE WILL BE
REWARDED SOON.
您的忍耐將很快獲得回報

In case of loss, please return to:

As a rew